To:

_____

From:

_____

Poppa Said . . .

Stop that, you're giving me a splitting headache!

RONNIE
SELLERS
PRODUCTIONS
-Gift Books-
PORTLAND, MAINE

Poppa said . . .

If all your friends
jumped off a cliff,
would you?

Poppa said . . .

Don't bite off more than you can chew.

Poppa said . . .

You don't have to yell,
I'm not deaf.

Poppa said . . .

Son, you may not be a
movie star, but you've
sure got what it takes.

Poppa said . . .

Quit your
clowning around.

Poppa said . . .

Nobody likes a crybaby.

Poppa said . . .

If you're looking for
the perfect man,
go to the movies.

Poppa said . . .

Stop that,
you're giving me a
splitting headache!

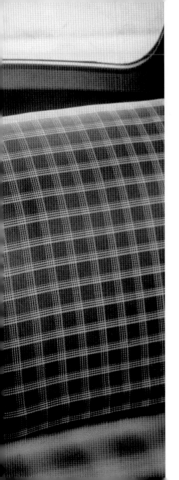

Poppa said . . .

If I have to stop this car . . . somebody's going to be sorry.

Poppa said . . .

If at first you don't succeed, try, try, again.

Poppa said . . .

Quit your daydreaming.

Poppa said . . .

Be careful, you're
skating on thin ice!

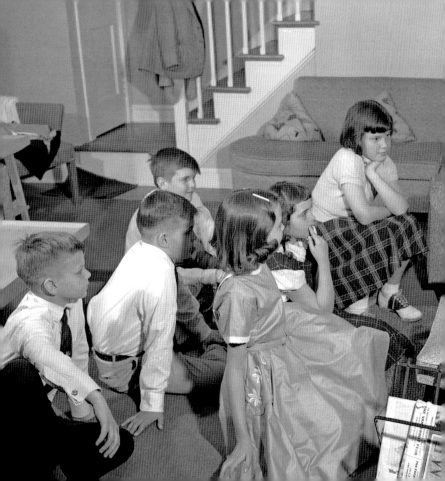

Poppa said . . .

Don't sit so close
to the TV, you'll
go blind.

29

Poppa said . . .

If you hang out
with hoodlums,
people are going
to think you're a
hoodlum, too.

Poppa said . . .

Everyone loves the dog
until it's time to feed him
or take him for a walk.

Poppa said . . .

Don't be afraid to
shoot for the stars.

Poppa said . . .

Sit up straight,
don't be a slouch.

Poppa said . . .

No pain,
no gain.

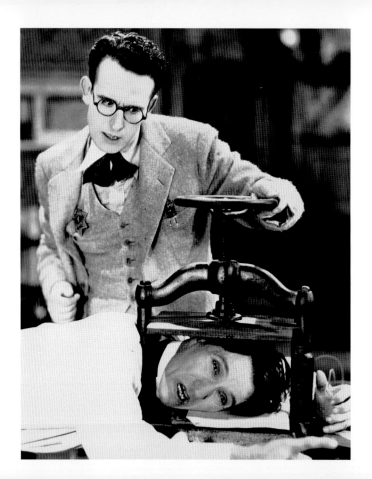

Poppa said . . .

You'd forget your head
if it wasn't attached.

Poppa said . . .

Don't cry over
spilled milk.

Poppa said . . .

Find someone who's going to support you and treat you like a queen.

Poppa said . . .

Nobody ever said
life was fair.

Poppa said . . .

How well do you know
this guy who's taking
you to the prom?

Poppa said . . .

Life has its ups
and downs.

Poppa said . . .

If wishes were horses,
beggars would ride.

Poppa said . . .

Look who got up on the wrong side of the bed!

Poppa said . . .

This place is like a
three ring circus!

Poppa said . . .

I'm sorry, but what you're saying just doesn't add up.

Poppa said . . .

Save your money for
a rainy day.

Poppa said . . .

What do I look like,
a bank?

Poppa said . . .

Tell the truth,
and you won't
get tangled up
in your own lies.

Poppa said . . .

Listen mister, if I've told
you once, I've told you
a thousand times. . .

Poppa said . . .

You can do anything
when you put your
mind to it.

Poppa said . . .

 How can you study
with all that racket?

Poppa said . . .

How many times do I have to tell you not to play on the stairs?

Poppa said . . .

You better not let me
catch you out of bed!

Poppa said . . .

If you lie down with
dogs, you'll wake
up with fleas.

Poppa said . . .

Always remember
to cover your butt.

Poppa said . . .

You kids are growing like weeds.

Poppa said . . .

 Don't give me that look!

Poppa said . . .

If you pull a stunt like that again,
I'll call the cops on you!

Poppa said . . .

Anyone who can eat as much as you do and still be skinny must have a hollow leg.

Poppa said . . .

Watch out! One of these days you're going to fall and break your neck.

Poppa said . . .

Be good or I'll sell
you to the gypsies.

Poppa said . . .

Hindsight is 20/20.

Poppa said . . .

First you must finish
your chores, then you
can go play.

Poppa said . . .

Don't put all your
eggs in one basket.

Poppa said . . .

It's not whether you win or lose that's important, it's how you play the game.

Poppa said . . .

Listen kid, I know you're going
to be famous someday,
but you still have to do
your homework.

Poppa said . . .

Remember, I'm the one
who's going to catch
you when you fall.

Poppa said . . .

A penny saved
is a penny earned.

Poppa said . . .

You kids never listen to a word I say!

Poppa said . . .

Go ask your mother.

Credits

Cover image: © Benelux Press/Retrofile.com

p. 2-3 photo © Benelux Press/Retrofile; pp.14-15 photo © Benelux Press/Retrofile; pp. 16-17 photo ©

Sasha/Getty Images; pp. 18-19 photo © Benelux Press/Retrofile; pp. 20-21 photo © John Chillingworth/Getty

images; p. 23 photo © Retrofile.com; p. 24 photo © Thurston Hopkins/Getty Images; p. 27 photo ©

Retrofile.com; pp. 28-29 photo © Retrofile.com; pp. 30-31 photo © Underwood Photo Archives/Superstock; p.

32 © photo © Superstock; p. 36 © photo © Retrofile.com; pp. 40-41 photo © Underwood Photo

Archives/Superstock; p. 43 photo © Retrofile.com; p. 44 photo © Underwood Photo Archives/Superstock; p. 47

photo © Retrofile.com; p. 48 photo © Evening Standard/Getty Images; p. 51 photo © Retrofile.com; pp. 52-53

photo © Thinkstock/Retrofile.com; p. 55 photo © Retrofile.com; pp 56-57 photo © American

Stock/Retrofile.com; p. 59 photo © Retrofile.com; p. 60 photo © Retrofile.com; p. 62 photo © Retrofile.com; pp.

64-65 photo © Underwood Photo Archives/Superstock; pp. 66-67 photo © Retrofile.com; p. 68 photo © B.

Taylor/Retrofile.com; p.71 photo © Thurston Hopkins/Getty Images; p. 73 © photo © Retrofile.com; p.74 photo

© Lambert/Archive PhotosGetty Images; pp. 76-77 photo © Corson/Retrofile.com; p. 79 photo © Superstock; p.

80 photo © Retrofile.com; p. 83 photo © Debrocke/Retrofile.com; p. 84 photo © Underwood Photo

*Our thanks to everyone at RSP, Inc.
who shared their favorite poppa sayings
with us for this book.*

Published by Ronnie Sellers Productions, Inc.

Copyright © 2004 Ronnie Sellers Productions, Inc.

P.O. Box 818, Portland, Maine 04104
For ordering information:
Phone: 1-800-MAKE-FUN (800-625-3386)
Fax: (207) 772-6814
Visit our Web site: www.makefun.com
E-mail: rsp@rsvp.com

Concept by Ronnie Sellers
Photo Editor: Mary Baldwin

ISBN: 1-56906-581-0

Printed and bound in China.

Cover image © Benelux Press/Retrofile.com